Contents

	Pages
The Basics	4-5
Smacking	6-7
Why Children Misbehave	8-9
Boundaries & Routines	10-11
Rewards	12-13
Copying & Guiding	14-15
Time-out	16-17
How to deal with...	18-23
Bedtime Routines	24-27
Toilet Training	28
Bed Wetting	29
Support	30-31

The Basics

A few simple points to get you started:

- **Be firm but fair**
  Children need clear guidance and boundaries to understand what is expected of them.

NO! You mustn't pull mummy's earring because it hurts!

- **Be consistent**
  Don't back track on what you say and do, mean what you say and stick to it. Being consistent helps your child to feel secure.

- **Focus on good behaviour**
  Encouraging good behaviour often works better than criticising bad behaviour. Children who are constantly told they are naughty are more likely to live up to that name.

Wow! Sweeth- that's fantasti-

- **Give praise**
  Your approval means a lot to your child. Show that you are excited about your child's accomplishments.

- **Don't hit**
  Physical punishment is never the answer, it makes any situation worse.

The Basics

Work together
A parent's job is easier when both parents share the responsibility of discipline, even if they don't live together. One parent shouldn't be seen as the 'bad guy'.

● **Love**
Ensure that your child always feels loved, even if they are behaving badly. It is the behaviour, not the child that is the problem.

Make time
The most precious gift that you can give your child is time. Make time to develop that special parent/child bond, and enjoy being together.

● **Remain calm**
Often easier said than done, but gives you a much better chance of dealing with a difficult situation successfully!

And remember, whilst parenting is the most wonderful experience in the world it can also be frustrating at times - **kids will test you - it's normal!**

Smacking

It is never acceptable to smack, hit, punch, shake or in any way physically harm your child as a form of punishment.

- Hitting or shaking can cause permanent damage to delicate young bodies.

NO!

- Children who are hit learn that it's okay to try to solve problems by hitting others.

Physical punishment:

- Doesn't teach respect for rules.

- Doesn't teach the correct way to behave.

- Does teach your child to be afraid of you.

Oh no! Please don't let her get mad!

Smacking

Hitting a child only shows that **you** have lost control.

If you are feeling angry or upset take time to cool off before disciplining your child.

Don't worry, it's normal to feel like this sometimes, but you must take time-out to regain control.

Turn to page 30 to find out more about developing your support network.

1...2...3...4...5 ...6...7...8...9

10!

Right, to your room until I decide what to do!

- **If you think that you might harm your child seek help immediately.**

Turn to page 31 for details of who you can contact for help.

Smacking never solves problems, in the long term it only makes them worse.

Read on to find out more about how to discipline your child in more positive ways that will benefit everyone.

Why Children Misbehave

Understanding why your child misbehaves can often be the key to helping you to deal with a situation effectively. Behaviour may be affected by:

- **Strong feelings** such as:
  - anger
  - anxiety
  - disappointment
  - fear
  - frustration
  - hurt
  - jealousy.

- **Physical problems** such as:
  - illness
  - hunger
  - tiredness.

RUMBLE
RUMBLE

- **Changes in routine** such as:
  - the birth of a new baby
  - a divorce or separation
  - moving to a new home
  - a parent returning to work.

Why Children Misbehave

Insecurity
Your child may worry about being alone, or be afraid of losing you, especially if they have already lost one parent.

Wants
Children can often become frustrated about not being able to have things that they want or do things for which they don't yet have the skills. They may also want more attention.

Confusion
This can be a particular problem if there is inconsistency in what you expect from your child, especially if there is more than one main carer with different rules.

Setting Boundaries

Boundaries and **routines** should be set to make everyone's lives easie
Make sure that your child knows why they are necessary.

- Don't just say 'NO', always explain why not.

- Remember to be consistent, changing the boundaries will confuse your child.

- Make sure that boundaries and consequences of crossing them are appropriate for your child's age.

Babies need to know that you will take care of them and keep them safe. Once babies start to crawl you will need to gently remove them from danger and explain why.

Setting Boundaries

Toy box rules!
1. Put your toys away when you have finished playing.
2. Play nicely and share your toys with your sister
3. Leave the play room as you found it!

Thankyou
MUM
x

Routines help to make your child feel secure and help to make your life run more smoothly, for example:

- Always have a baby changing bag ready for when you go out. Restock it when you return from an outing.

Shopping List!
1. Oranges.
2. Eggs
3. Washing powder
4. Carrots
5. Peas
6. Salad
7. Nappies.

This Week's Menu!
Mon - Pasta Bolognese
Tues - Tuna Salad
Wed - Beef Stew
Thurs - Fish Pie
Fri - Stir Fry
Sat - Chicken Korma
Sun - Sunday Roast

- Plan meals and keep an ongoing shopping list.

- Prepare clothes and school bags the night before.

- Don't try and do too many things in too short a time.

Be prepared

- Organized routines mean that your child knows what is expected.

- If you are in control your child will pick up your positive vibes.

- If you are stressed your child is far more likely to misbehave.

Rewards

Rewards can be used to show that your child is succeeding and that you are pleased when they succeed, it also shows your child that doing well is fun.

Rewards are:

You must decide which rewards work best for the different things you want your child to do. Give positive attention when your child has done something that you are pleased with.

Rewards

hings to remember when rewarding children:

- Reward them as soon as they do what you want them to do.

- At first, reward every time they try to do what you want.

- Reward less often as they find it easier to do something.

- Always praise them (or give hugs, kisses or smiles).

- Always say exactly why you are pleased with them.

- Don't promise rewards that you can't give.

> Good girl! Well done for putting all the bricks away after your game.
> I'm so pleased!

Rewards should be 100% positive

If a child is behaving badly, you can remove things that he/she enjoys, but don't take away rewards that have been given for good behaviour.

> I told you not to pull your sister's hair and you carried on! So now I'm taking your fire engine away until you can show me you can behave nicely.

Copying and Guiding

Copying

Children learn from watching **other children** and also from watching y...

Encourage your child to watch other children doing what you would like your child to do. Use praise and encouragement.

Set a good example

- Listen to your child and it will encourage your child to listen to you.

- Speak to your child in the way that you would like to be spoken to.

- Don't be violent or aggressive or your child will think that it is an acceptable way to behave.

- Sit down together at the table to eat. It's the best way to encourage good eating habits.

Watch for the green man!

- Don't dash across the road, if you want your child to understand the importance of crossing safely.

Copying and Guiding

Guiding

Children need to be guided into doing what you want them to do.

- Use small steps to begin with.
- Give lots of encouragement.
- Focus on positive achievements.
- Have patience with difficulties.
- Reward them when they have succeeded.

Offer your child a choice

This encourages your child to cooperate, as he/she is able to make a decision whilst still following your guidance.

For example:

It's time for bed. Do you want me to read you a story on the sofa or in bed?

It's cold today. Do you want to wear the green jumper or the red one?

Shall we tidy up the bricks first or the crayons?

Time-out

Ignoring

It's often best to ignore annoying behaviour as some children enjoy the attention they get from misbehaving.

- Make sure your child knows from the start why you are ignoring him/her.

- Do not keep telling your child off as you are giving him/her attention and not controlling the situation.

- Ignore your child everytime he/she plays up.

- Ensure that your child does not get attention from anyone else.

This course of action could make your child's behaviour worse to begin with, but it should improve if you persist.

Remember to make sure that your child is safe.

You can't go to Joe's house now because it's too late. When you calm down and stop making that silly noise, I will talk to Joe's mummy about going to play tomorrow.

If ignoring doesn't work then you may need to try **time-out** which means removing your child from the place where he/she is misbehaving.

Time-out

Time-out gives your child a chance to calm down and think about his/her behaviour.

Stay firm and explain to your child what is happening.

Put your child in a place where there is nothing much to do, not in a room full of toys which could be seen as a reward.

Make sure that your child is safe.

> You need to sit here until you have calmed down. When you are ready to say 'sorry' and share the toys nicely, you can go back to play with the others.

Your child must be old enough to understand what is happening so that he/she can learn from the situation.

Don't leave your child for too long - as a guide, one minute for each year of your child's age.

> Well Done!!! You calmed down much quicker today!

- After time-out, talk to your child to explain why his/her behaviour was unacceptable.

- Encourage your child to apologise, but don't insist.

- Repeat time-out as many times as necessary.

- Praise your child at the first opportunity.

- Be consistent.

How to deal with...

Temper tantrums

Stay calm and help your child to regain control.

Try the following methods, you will soon get to know which method(s) works best for your child.

- Ignore the tantrum.

- Hold your child close.

Shhhhhh, it's okay

- Leave the scene, but only if it's safe to do so.

- Offer a distraction.

- Listen to your child and be sympathetic.

Don't give in or offer a treat if the tantrum stops.

Hmmm, maybe if I scream for long enough she'll buy me an ice-cream, like she did last week to shut me up!

BE CONSISTENT

How to deal with...

ggression - tting, biting, scratching, nipping

Never hit, bite, scratch or nip your child back.

Explain to your child why this behaviour is not acceptable.

If your child has been agressive towards another child remove your child until he/she has calmed down.

> NO! You mustn't hit mummy, because it hurts me and it certainly won't make me buy you any sweets!

> See, it's a much nicer game when you all take turns!

- When your child has calmed down make sure that he/she says 'sorry'.

- Help your child to find words to express his/her feelings.

- Teach your child how to solve problems peacefully, such as taking turns.

Younger children may bite, hit, scratch or nip when they are excited or seeking attention. Make sure your child knows from day one that this type of behaviour is not acceptable and teach him/her how to ask for attention.

BE CONSISTENT

19

How to deal with...

Lying

- Always tell the truth - children learn by example.

- Expect your child to tell the truth.

- Emphasise the importance of trust.

- Explain the consequences of lying.

> It's really important that you always tell me the truth about where you are going, so I know you are safe.

> I'm very pleased you came and told me about this straight away, but you shouldn't really have been playing with my make-up should you?

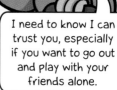

> I need to know I can trust you, especially if you want to go out and play with your friends alone.

- Stay calm when your child admits a mistake.

- Praise your child for telling the truth, even if the truth means admitting to having done something bad.

BE CONSISTENT

How to deal with...

Swearing

Watch your own language - children learn by example.

Teach your child that there are better words that can be used other than swear words.

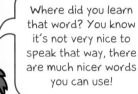

Where did you learn that word? You know it's not very nice to speak that way, there are much nicer words you can use!

Talking back

- Avoid unnecessary confrontation by giving your child choices.

- Try not to get into an argumentative situation.

- Explain why calmly and firmly.

- Don't shout.

- If necessary ignore your child until he/she can speak to you politely.

BE CONSISTENT

How to deal with...

Stealing

- Never steal or borrow without permission - children learn by example.

- Teach young children to understand ownership.

- Explain to your child the possible consequences of taking other people's things.

How would you feel if somebody took your new bike?

That wouldn't be fair cos it's mine!

I'm sorry I took some sweets without asking Nana.

I promise I won't do it again.

- Ensure that your child returns what is not his/hers and says "sorry".

- Encourage older children to explain their actions. Stealing can sometimes be the result of other problems.

- Don't let your child see stealing as a way of getting attention. Deal with the situation firmly but quietly.

BE CONSISTENT

How to deal with...

Sibling rivalry

Never compare one child to another.

Make your child feel loved for the person that he/she is.

Let your child know that he/she is a valued member of the family.

Tell your children 'I love you' often.

Why can't you be more like your brother? He would never do a thing like that!

NO!

I'll just put Stacey to bed and read her a story, then you and I can read a chapter from your book before bed if you'd like?

- Encourage older children to help with a new baby so that they don't feel excluded.

- Make special time to spend with each child individually.

- Make sure that everyone understands the family rules.

- Explain why some rules are different depending on the age or needs of different family members.

BE CONSISTENT

Bedtime Routines

Bedtime routines for babies

Night time feeds

Make a regular routine of 'back to bed' after night time feeds.

After about 6 months old, a baby should not need food or drink during the night. Try to stop night feeds or drinks around this age, as they could become habits that are difficult to break.

A crying baby who needs settling

Babies vary in how much they cry, but you will soon learn what is normal for your child.

Try these ideas to settle your baby:

- Attend straight away.

- Change your baby's nappy if necessary.

- If you use a dummy, replace it.

- Pat your baby gently and make soothing noises or play soft music.

- Leave your baby for a few minutes and return to comfort again if necessary, repeat until your baby is soothed.

Bedtime Routines

on't leave your baby to cry for a long time.

owever, if you pick up your baby too soon he/she may learn to cry just ⌐ be picked up. Seek advice from your health visitor if the ideas in the st opposite don't help.

aps

- Not all children need a nap but some may need two.

- If your child is drowsy, let him/her nap but preferably early in the day.

- If bedtime is 7pm for example try to avoid a teatime nap.

- Some children have to learn good sleeping habits, they are important for both of you, so set the rules and stick to them.

Bedtime Routines

Bedtime routines for toddlers

Having a bedtime routine is important for you and your child.

- A bedtime routine encourages a child to fall asleep easily.

- A routine could include having a bath, followed by a story and a cuddle.

- Settle your child in bed, not on the sofa or in your bed.

- Make sure that everyone sticks to the planned routine.

- Don't make a plan that you know you won't be able to keep.

Once your child is in bed and asleep you can have some time for yourself.

If your child wakes and cries:

- Check that he/she is okay.

- Settle him/her down again.

- Leave.

- Return after a few minutes and repeat until your child has settled

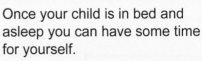

Bedtime Routines

emember:

Bedtime is not a punishment, it should be a happy relaxed time.

Lots of activity before bed doesn't tire children out, it just makes them over excited.

If you don't stick to your routine, your child may feel cheated out of your special time together and play up as a result.

your children get out of bed, put them back in their own beds. Don't put
nem in your bed or bring them downstairs or they may want to do this
very night! Make it clear that their excuses won't change the routine.
'ou may have to do this many times at first until they get used to the
dea.

- If your child is going to bed late, try bringing the bed time forward by half an hour each night. A child who is tired is more likely to misbehave.

- A dim light may help if your child is afraid of the dark.

Toilet Training

Introduce the potty/toilet at each nappy change so that your child understands what it's for.

Take advice from your health visitor on what is the correct age to start toilet training.

- Plan a time to start when you are going to be at home and you know that you can spend some time training your child.

- Use pants, not a nappy. Your child needs to be able to remove his/her own pants to use the potty or toilet

- Encourage your child to sit on the potty or toilet but don't leave him/her for a long time.

- Give lots of praise and encouragement.

- Be patient, don't make potty training a battle.

- If it's not working try again at a later date.

Accidents

- Help to avoid accidents by reminding your child to visit the toilet before going out and at regular intervals during the day.

- Always carry a spare pair of pants, so that little accidents can be sorted without any fuss. Being angry with your child won't help.

Bed Wetting

ed wetting

Deal with a wet bed promptly, but don't make an issue of it.

Reassure your child, don't be cross.

Wash or bath your child.

Strip the bed and wash the bedding. A waterproof under sheet will help to protect the bed and make cleaning up easier.

Praise your child if he/she has a dry bed.

- If bed wetting persists you may need to ask your GP, Health Visitor or School Nurse for advice.
Your GP may check to see if your child has a water infection.

Sometimes children become upset about something that's happening in their lives, and this can result in bed-wetting. At these times your child will need extra reassurance and settling.

Support

Don't expect to be the perfect parent all the time.

All parents need support from other people.

Your support network may include:

- Family
- Friends
- Neighbours
- Health Visitors/ School Nurses
- Doctors
- Teachers
- Community Leaders

Family, friends and neighbours can be a great source of informal advice, providing a listening ear, hands on practical help and of course babysitting.

Your health visitor, school nurse or doctor will always be there to provide professional advice and support, and can also introduce you to other support networks in your area.

Try these great places to meet other parents:

- Sure Start Children's Centres
- Parenting Groups
- Toddler Groups
- Single Parent Groups

Remember, it is important to make time for you.
If you are tired and stressed, your parenting skills will be compromised and both you and your child will suffer.

Support

on't struggle alone!

sk for help if you need it, you owe it to your child.

'e all need to feel loved and cared for - children **and** adults.

n case of an accident, emergency or just dvice these are some useful numbers to ng for information and help.

HS England   tel: 111   www.nhsdirect.nhs.uk

HS Direct
/ales   tel: 0845 4647   www.nhsdirect.wales.nhs.uk

HS 24 (Scotland)   tel: 08454 24 24 24   www.nhs24.com

ure Start
hildren's Centres   www.gov.uk/find-sure-start-childrens-centre

our local Health Visitor can be contacted via your GP practice.

Add your GP's phone number here

Other numbers in your area:

Caring for Kids

Over 1/4 million copies sold nationwide!

'Positive Parenting', the 7th book in the 'Caring for Kids' ser
is an essential, easy-to-follow guide for all parents and carers
gives clear advice on how best to manage your child's behavio

From temper tantrums...

...to hugs and kiss

Parenting is hard work, but it's fun and rewarding, enjoy it!

Positive Parenting has been developed in association with:

B̲urnett Fields
Children & Family Centre

A Sure Start Children's Centre

42 Greaves Street,
Little Horton, Bradford,
BD5 7PE
Tel: 01274 436500

Also available:

www.kidpremiership.com

ISBN 9781906036584

📞 01484 668008   📠 01484 668009   ✉ mail@kidpremiership.com
One17ED, The Dyehouse, Armitage Bridge, Huddersfield, HD4 7PD

9 781906 036584 >